Noah's Last Canoe

Great Plains Publications
420 – 70 Arthur Street
Winnipeg, MB R3B 1G7
www.greatplains.mb.ca

Great Plains Publications gratefully acknowledges the financial support provided for its publishing program
by the Government of Canada through the Book Publishing Industry Development Program (BPIDP);
the Canada Council for the Arts; as well as the Manitoba Department of Culture, Heritage and Tourism;
and the Manitoba Arts Council.

Design & Typography by Relish Design Studio Inc.
Printed in Canada by Friesens

LIBRARY AND ARCHIVES CANADA CATALOGUING IN PUBLICATION

Evans, Doug
      Noah's last canoe : the lost art of Cree birch bark canoe building / Doug Evans

ISBN 978-1-894283-82-3

      1. Canoes and canoeing—Design and construction. 2. Cree Indians—Manitoba—Boats.
3. Boatbuilding. I. Title.
E99.C88E93 2008   623.82'9   C2008-902492-3

NOAH'S LAST CANOE

Doug Evans

GREAT PLAINS
PUBLICATIONS

The canoe
is a treasure come down
to us from a rich
and ancient culture.

INTRODUCTION

The large stands of birch trees (*Betula papyrifera*) found throughout Canada's boreal forest were traditionally highly prized by First Nations communities. According to northern Cree Elders, their use can be traced to the beginnings of time when powerful spiritual beings endowed the tree with its characteristic stripes, its Thunderbird markings and its exceptional properties. In fact, many northern Indigenous cultures throughout the world have regarded the birch tree as a sacred plant that was blessed with special qualities for the benefit of humankind. The traditional harvesting of its bark, leaves, wood, roots and the bracket fungus (*Fomis fomentarius*) which is parasitic to the birch and served as tinder, was a "holy undertaking" accompanied with great reverence and prayer offerings.

The use of the bark wrapping of the birch spanned the lifetime of an individual – from birth, when the bark served as a cradle cover, to death, when it functioned as a wrapping for the deceased. The fact that the bark can be peeled to any desired thickness, stored for long periods of time and regenerated for future use – along with its light weight, portability, durability and strength – all resulted in its extensive use. The northern Cree manufactured a number of items from the bark including lodge coverings, containers for food and personal items, hunting and fishing gear, wrappings for medicines, tinder, torches, patterned transparencies, and backing for bead work. The bark also served as a documentary medium for the communication of camp locations and the transmission of sacred rites, songs and teachings passed down by the Old Ones from time immemorial. Healing beverages were brewed from the tree's bark, leaves and twigs. Its wood was used to make a variety of utensils.

Of all the objects that were made from birch trees, it is the birch bark canoe that has gained recognition and admiration throughout the world. The birch bark canoe is a unique example of the engineering skills of First Nations peoples. For communities who depended upon hunting, gathering and fishing for their survival, the bark canoe was an ideal vehicle of transportation along the vast systems of waterways that linked seasonal camping and hunting grounds.

With the arrival of Europeans in North America, its value was quickly recognized and the birch bark canoe was soon adopted as a major vehicle for moving people and goods during the open-water seasons. By the mid-1700s, canoe-building had become an established industry at certain major settlements and fur trade posts. It was used by a wide range of Euro-Americans including explorers, missionaries, scientists, government agents, Victorian "tourists" and sportsmen before it was replaced with the canvas-covered version. By the turn of the 20th century, the first wood-canvas canoe was constructed for the fur trade in the James Bay area where local Cree builders used modified birch bark canoe-style techniques. For example, tacks and bolts, bindings and fastenings were made from local spruce roots. Over time, the canvas canoe predominated.

Traditionally, the specialized skills and knowledge required by Aboriginal canoe-makers involved years of both observation and experience. In addition to technical skills needed to produce this lightweight, resilient, strong and hydrodynamic craft, the builders possessed an intimate understanding of the properties of birch bark and other construction materials gathered off the land, such as various woods, resins, and roots for sewing. Canoe-building was a labour-intensive project involving the support of a network of relatives and their expertise. Men, women and older children participated in various aspects of the preparation and building processes, their respective work skills complementing one another. The manufacture of canoes was a seasonal task, incorporated into late spring/early summer work activities when the bark of the birch trees was more pliable and easily removed. Various sizes of the craft were made according to function. Smaller canoes were used for hunting and trapping, while larger versions of 4.26 to 4.87 metres (14 to 16 feet) transported entire families and their belongings.

While canoe construction among the northern Cree has been previously documented in historical writings and anthropological studies, there are still few detailed visual recordings of the actual step-by-step production of one. When G. Garth Taylor produced the 1980 publication "Canoe Construction in a Cree Cultural Tradition" for the Canadian Ethnology Service, National Museums of Canada, he noted in his preface that there were few Cree who could build a canoe in a traditional manner and "even fewer who can recall the myths, songs and other cultural associations which were once an integral part of the builder's craft." In his publication, Taylor recorded the production of a canvas canoe by the eastern Cree of Great Whale River on the east side of Hudson Bay in Quebec. To date, Noah Custer's birch bark canoe is a unique product of an ancient craft that was used by the Cree who resided in the regions of northeastern Saskatchewan and northwestern Manitoba.

Doug Evans' account of Noah Custer's birch bark canoe reveals the persistence of the traditional methods of construction within a woodlands Cree family residing in northeastern Saskatchewan. It is of interest to note that both the building of the canoe and the writing of this publication were accomplished through retrospective efforts. That is, as a young man, Noah had helped his parents build their canoes, but had never actually made one himself. Therefore, the canoe produced for The Manitoba Museum was reconstructed from his memory and from that of his wife, Emma. In the same vein, Evans had never formally written up his fieldnotes for public record, so his observations also have a retrospective aspect – made possible by his impressive ability to recall minute details and his willingness to share his photographic documentation of the project through this publication. Evans has generously donated copies of his photographs to The Manitoba Museum.

As is evident in his several biographically-based popular publications, Evans is an astute observer of life and detail. Although his account of canoe-building is technical in nature, it is intended for a general audience. His intent is to guide readers through the complexities of the preparatory work and the actual construction process in an easily understood manner. The carefully organized descriptions are complemented with field photographs of every stage of manufacture. The tone of Evans' writing reveals his closeness to and respect for the Custer family. Throughout, he clearly reveals his tremendous appreciation for the achievements of northern Cree culture. His remarks relative to the challenges faced by the Custer family as they worked through the project make the reader's experience "real" and personable. Clearly, we are not only being given a glimpse into how an object was made from a technical aspect, but also the lifestyle of a Cree family residing in the north during the middle of the 20th century.

Until the 1960s, The Manitoba Museum did not have professional anthropologists on staff to research the cultures and histories of First Nations peoples, or to collect representative artifacts for study and exhibit-development. Since the late 1930s, the majority of the Museum's Aboriginal artifact holdings had been acquired as private donations and loans as well as through purchase.

By the late 1960s, Jack Herbert, the Museum's Director at that time, undertook to contact local collectors residing in various parts of the province to help build up the institution's collections base. This endeavour was likely made in anticipation of the relocation of the Museum to its new modernized and largely expanded collections/exhibitions facility on Main Street.

It would be the beginning of project-related field ethnography that would support exhibits in the newly planned permanent galleries.

While the Museum's records on the subject of early ethnographic field collecting are not extensive, we do know that Herbert had been in contact with Harry Moody, a storeowner at Denare Beach, Saskatchewan (just west of Flin Flon, Manitoba) who worked very closely with the northern Cree of the area. An avocational archaeologist, ethnographer and historian, Moody accumulated an extensive collection that he eventually housed at the Northern Gateway Museum which he founded in 1957. Moody himself assisted The Manitoba Museum with its northern Cree collection in the 1960s by donating several birch bark transparencies (small sections of bark into which designs have been bitten) that were produced by Angelique Merasty and her mother.

Moody reported to Herbert the northern collecting activities of another local individual, Doug Evans. Evans, also an avocational heritage enthusiast, resided in Flin Flon. He "mentored" under Moody, and while employed with the federal Department of Manpower, he was in a position to visit a number of northern communities and to speak with local Elders about their history and culture. Herbert had met Evans in 1956 and described him as an "enthusiastic" and "vigorous" person of "integrity."

By the time he formally contacted the Museum in early 1968, he informed Herbert that he had already collected four hours of taped recollections on the subjects of canoe-building, food preparation and storage, child-bearing, the construction of sturgeon-skin jars, and the preparation of traditional medicines. In addition to offering his services for fieldwork, Evans proposed contracting Elders to produce a number of traditional types of articles including a drum, a sturgeon skin storage jar and a tikanogan (cradleboard). The construction process was to be documented through photography and oral history.

Although there had been some discussion regarding the possibility of a partnership with the Department of Anthropology at the University of Manitoba, for various reasons this arrangement did not materialize. Therefore, Evans was asked to work solely on behalf of The Manitoba Museum. During the period 1968-1969, Evans acquired and documented several locally-made artifacts and recorded oral histories with the assistance of Elders and community translators. Objects were collected from Brochet, Granite Lake, Nelson House, and Pukatawagan. Noah Custer and his wife produced the largest collection. They made baskets, a pair of snowshoes, a fish net, a dog harness, a dog whip, a spruce gum sieve, bone knives, bone pipes, a cradleboard and recreational articles including a violin and pin-and-cup game. In July, 1968, Richard Conn, then Chief of the Division of Human History, approved expenses for Noah's construction of the 4.8 metre (16-foot) birch bark canoe that is featured in this publication.

Owing to a commitment by several parties in the heritage sector, there has been a movement since the 1970s to document and revive the skills required to construct traditional forms of Canadian Aboriginal watercraft. The work of a number of Indigenous canoe-builders has been recorded, and some of this material has been published, displayed in museums and promoted by historical societies and other interest groups. In some First Nations communities, the information associated with canoe building serves an even greater purpose – that of regenerating cultural awareness and instilling pride in an ancient and rich heritage.

On behalf of The Manitoba Museum, I would like to express my appreciation to the Custer family and to Doug Evans for ensuring that the information generated through the construction of Noah's canoe will be publicly accessible and preserved for future generations.

Dr. Katherine Pettipas
Curator of Ethnology and the HBC Museum Collection
The Manitoba Museum

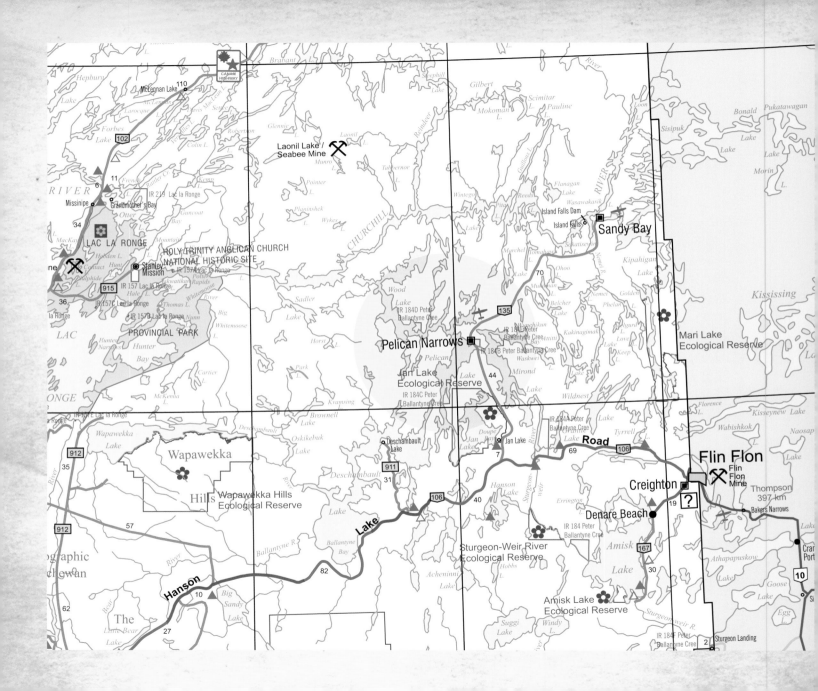

History, as written by the Europeans who settled in North America, has always given the impression that the wonders of technology they brought with them astonished and delighted the people they found populating the country. This is true, but only to a degree. Europeans brought with them tools, equipment and methods that allowed the original people to jump—in one generation—from the Stone age to the Iron age. What those histories often fail to give sufficient emphasis to is the fact that those first Europeans felt the same astonishment and delight when they encountered some of the technology of the Aboriginal peoples.

Methods of living in ultra-cold conditions, methods of avoiding scurvy, methods of harvesting and preserving food supplies and an established trading system that covered most of North America are only some of the accomplishments of the First Peoples. There is one technological achievement, however, that stands out above all the rest and that is the bark canoe.

With the exception of the awkward hide-covered round boats of the Welsh and Irish, most European watercraft were wooden and heavy. They were subject to rot and waterlog and required considerable power, oar or sail, to propel. Imagine what went through the minds of the first European seamen to encounter bark canoes. Here was a vessel that was resistant to rot and water-logging, required no painting or annual caulking, and could be repaired with what was at hand in the countryside. It was a craft whose basic design could be adapted to a variety of sizes and uses. It did not require heavy oars or sails for propulsion, but, due to its long slender shape, could move through the water quickly and silently using only light paddles.

With the exception of some desert and mountain areas, the North American continent at the time of the arrival of the first Europeans was a country linked by water. A network of streams, ponds, lakes and rivers made travel by water the natural method of transport. The lakes varied in size from inland seas to small ponds. The moving water could be huge rivers like the Mississippi or tiny creeks only a few feet wide. The canoe was a wonderful response to all of these challenges. It was agile enough to navigate the smallest of creeks and, properly managed, could be relied upon even in fairly rough conditions on the lakes. Much the same building technique was used to produce the trapper's small canoe as was used in building larger ones designed to hold a whole family and their belongings. When the voyageurs began to use canoes to move freight from Montreal into the far Northwest, they used the same basic building method to produce canoes capable of carrying a number of tons.

At one time each tribe had its own distinct design of bark canoe. A practiced eye could easily tell a northen woodland Cree canoe from one built by the Dene (Chipewyan). Some of the differences were matters of style, it is true, but most of the variations of design reflected adaptations to the river and lake conditions in the area of the tribe. One of the most remarkable things about the birch bark canoe was that they did not have to be built by specially-trained boat builders. First Nations families in need of a canoe, following traditional methods, could produce a canoe in two or three weeks.

Later, when the canvas-over-cedar-frame canoes became so cheap and easily obtainable that bark canoes were abandoned, museums began to take an interest in preserving the bark canoe in all its forms.

As of the 1960s, the Manitoba Museum in Winnipeg did not have an example of the type of canoe that was made by the northern Woodland Cree. No one knew of any original canoes that had survived so it was determined that one would have to be built. The problem was that, although there was no shortage of people who knew how to build a bark canoe, no one could be sure that they would be building to original Woodland Cree design.

Noah's Last Canoe

In 1967, I was living in Flin Flon, Manitoba and doing some volunteer work for The Manitoba Museum as a collector. I heard about the difficulty they were having in acquiring a true Cree canoe. During my travels around the northern reserves I had met a remarkable man named Noah Custer. I thought that if anyone knew how to build a canoe in the traditional style, it would be Noah.

In the old days, most of the Cree people lived the greatest part of the year on territory which had traditionally belonged to their clan or family. They would migrate through these areas, moving from place to place to take advantage of moose to be found in the fall in the swampy areas, fish runs in the spring, and deep protective forests in the winter. Later, when the fur trade became more organized, these traditional hunting and gathering areas changed to include areas that could produce saleable fur. For many years people lived on the 'trap lines', coming into the trading posts at certain times of the year to trade their furs, to visit and celebrate traditional gatherings.

Over a period of some years people gradually began to give up their life of moving around their hunting areas with the seasons and settled in villages. There were a number of factors involved in the First Nations people deciding to make this change, and it did not happen everywhere at once.

Noah

Emma

Peter

Anna

Noah Custer grew up in the old tradition, living on the family trap line year round with only periodic visits to the trading post at Pelican Narrows in Saskatchewan. When the Cree people began to move into permanent homes on the reserves, Noah and his wife Emma decided to continue to live in the old way. They did not move onto the reserve at Pelican Narrows with other members of the band, but continued to live a traditional lifestyle, moving around a large area, fishing in season, hunting moose and other game, harvesting what grew on the land as their parents and ancestors had done.

The Museum agreed that I should approach Noah with the idea of building a traditional Cree canoe. I was told not to discuss any matters of style or design with him as the Museum did not want anything other than Noah's memories to influence his work.

NOAH'S LAST CANOE

The Custer summer camp was on the east side of the Sturgeon Weir River near Leaf Rapids, about sixty miles west of Flin Flon, Manitoba. Noah lived there with his wife Emma. Son Peter and daughter Anna were frequent visitors. Their summer home was a cotton-wall tent of the type that has been used for years in the North. The camp was near the water and Noah had a net in the river which supplied them with a reliable source of fish.

Noah and Emma took great pride in demonstrating traditional skills, both to young First Nations people and other visitors. Bark baskets, snowshoes, willow bark fishing nets, and finely carved wooden spoons became very sought after. Emma would decorate the baskets by stitching dyed spruce roots into the bark much like decorative embroidery. Some of her baskets can be seen today in The Manitoba Museum in Winnipeg. Noah's most popular products were very detailed models of the traditional Woodland Cree bark canoe. These canoes were made with fine attention to detail, with every seam and rib an exact reproduction of the canoes Noah's parents had built and used when he was a child. Two examples are on display at the Northern Gateway Museum at Denare Beach, Saskatchewan.

Noah's Last Canoe

Noah agreed to build a full-sized sixteen-foot Cree canoe for the Museum. Apart from the length, he was given no other specifications as the Museum wanted to be sure that the canoe was a purely Cree canoe, uninfluenced by any other design. Although Noah had never constructed his own canoe, as a boy he had helped his parents build their own canoes. Both he and Emma had learned the traditional methods of building which was very evident when the actual work started. Each one seemed to know, without much discussion, exactly what to do and when to do it as the work went on.

The first step in the building process was the construction of a frame that would eventually make up the gunnels of the canoe.

Long slender pines of the type that grow in densely wooded stands were cut and hauled into the camp. Noah carefully peeled them and then used his axe to split them end-to-end creating long boards about three quarters of an inch thick that were again split lengthwise to produce pieces to form the gunnels of the canoe. At each point along the gunnels, where the thwarts would be set, Noah cut a square hole into the wood.

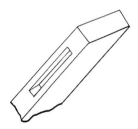

Great care was taken to get the frame exactly right as the final shape and performance of the canoe would depend on it. Noah referred to this frame as the 'back bone' of the canoe. If it was straight, then the canoe would 'swim straight'.

Wider boards were set aside to become the thwarts. Each thwart was trimmed back on the ends to produce a small tongue. When the two ends of the pair of gunnels were brought together, the pressure locked the thwarts into the prepared holes. Until the ribs were installed, the pressure of the bent frame would be enough to hold the thwarts in place. When the thwarts were first made up, they each had two or three holes bored into them close to the end. This was another indication that the Custers were working to an age-old step by step plan, because these holes would not actually be used till late in the building process. When the binding that held the bark hull to the frame was put on, it would lock the thwarts in place.

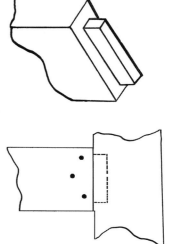

While Noah was working on the frame, Anna started gathering the spruce roots needed for sewing the bark. The traditional bark canoe had no nails or metal fasteners used in its construction. Spruce roots were used to bind the bark hull to the frame and to stitch together the pieces of bark that make up the hull. Split spruce roots are remarkably flexible for sewing. On drying they harden into wood, so there is no need to use any locking stitches or worry about the stitching coming loose.

The roots of the spruce were preferred as they are easy to peel and when fresh will split easily into long flexible lengths.

A damp mossy area in a thick grove of trees is best for root harvesting. Spruce send out a network of slender roots just below the surface. It was said that the longer the branches of the tree, the longer its roots would be. It takes a bit of patience to tease out a long strand but the roots are remarkably even in diameter, and very strong and flexible. The roots that have red tinted bark are preferred as the roots with old black bark are less flexible.

The person harvesting roots would first feel around in the moss near the drip ring of a tree to find a root of the right size, then peel as much of the moss away from the root as possible and, following its course among all the other roots, carefully extract it from the ground. Lengths of root up to five or six feet are not uncommon, so a good day of root gathering would produce enough for building a canoe.

Freshly harvested roots are not of even moistness so they were coiled into a pail and covered with water. Usually the whole collection of roots was not peeled and split all at once. Sewing with roots is slow work and the split root gets very stiff as it dries, so Emma would only peel and split enough roots for the sewing she intended to do that day. In this photo a piece of fresh root has been peeled to give an idea of how flexible they are.

Noah's next job was harvesting the birch bark he would require for the project. Because beavers are constantly harvesting birch trees that grow anywhere near the water, large specimens are usually found at a bit of distance from the lake.

Birch trees can grow to a considerable thickness but in the northern forests a tree about eight inches in diameter is not too hard to find and will yield sections of bark large enough for canoe building. The design of the bark canoe is such that a skilled builder can produce a canoe even when the only trees available are quite small.

The best birch bark is on the section of the tree below the first branches, although there are always sections that can't be used because of old knot holes or places where the bark has been damaged. Noah was very particular about the quality of the bark, inspecting each tree carefully and marking out the useful sections with his axe. If done carefully, the bark needed for canoe building and basket making can be removed from a birch tree without killing the tree, leaving the brown inner bark behind. In those instances where it was necessary to cut the tree down, Noah commented that you could never have enough dry firewood.

Noah used his axe to cut a deep groove in the bark parallel to the trunk. Wedging the blade of the axe into this cut, he slowly peeled the bark away from the wood. This operation has to be done carefully to prevent the bark from splitting. Once harvested, the sheets of bark were placed, outer bark up, in the water at the edge of the water. A few stones prevented the sheets from floating. The bark remained flexible for a very long time but it is easier to work with if it does not dry out too much.

Whether a canoe lasted for years or a new one built every spring depended on a number of circumstances. The nomadic lifestyle of the First Nations people in those days meant that canoes used in summer were often left at a point far away from the spring camp. Also bark canoes would often dry out and split in the intense dry cold of northern winters. One of the best ways to protect a canoe from drying out in the winter was to bury them, but burying the canoes in the fall wasn't always possible in the rocky Shield country. Building a canoe was only a matter of a couple of weeks work with the whole family working on it and, as it happens, the best time to harvest bark is in the spring when the sap is running.

When he was ready to start building, Noah cleared and carefully leveled a plot of ground about the size the canoe was to be. Then he collected about twenty heavy rocks. The bark was laid on the ground with the old outer layer facing up and the joints where the slabs met overlapping by and inch or so.

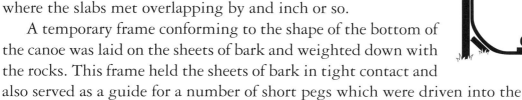

A temporary frame conforming to the shape of the bottom of the canoe was laid on the sheets of bark and weighted down with the rocks. This frame held the sheets of bark in tight contact and also served as a guide for a number of short pegs which were driven into the ground so that the bark was forced into an upward curve conforming to the frame.

Because the pieces of bark were not joined together but only held in position by the temporary frame, it was possible to move them enough to accommodate the curves of the canoe that were outlined by the short pegs. The amount of overlap at the joints then varied according to the curve required at that point, but this excess was later trimmed off.

NOAH'S LAST CANOE

The already-built main frame, which would become the gunnels of the canoe, then had to be put in place. A number of stakes were driven into the ground in a pattern matching this frame. The depth of the canoe was then established by tying the main frame to these upright sticks. By tying the middle of the canoe to the stakes first and then working out toward the ends, Noah was able to bend the pliable green wood into a sweeping upward curve at each end, with a slight upward bow near the middle.

Slowly and with infinite patience, Noah and Emma worked the bark up between the sticks and the frame. Little by little the bark began to take on the shape of a canoe. Bark, even after soaking in water, is stiff and has a tendency to curl up. It was interesting to note that the bark was used 'inside out'. Noah explained that if the bark was turned the other way, the natural tendency of the bark to resume its old shape would make it almost impossible to work with.

At this point the bark was held in position by being pressed between the upright stakes and the frame. This requires a fair amount of pressure and here Noah demonstrated the first of many pieces of ancient technology. The long upright stakes projected a foot or two above the frame after it had been set in place. The stakes were set along the outline of the canoe in pairs. Using twine made of long strands of willow bark twisted together, Noah and Emma tied each pair of stakes together. A stick was inserted between the two strands of bark rope, and it was twisted to pull the stakes tight against the frame, forcing the bark into position and holding it there.

Noah spent a great deal of time carefully preparing the ground where the canoe was going to be built. All bits of stone and small sticks were scraped away and small humps levelled out. This care right at the start insured that that canoe would have a straight and level bottom when it was finished, and also insured that no pebble or root would be driven up through the bark when the stones were piled on the interior frame.

Once the long upright stakes were in place, Noah and Emma spent most of the afternoon tugging and twisting the sheets of bark, getting them to fit as tightly together as possible.

It was now time to start sewing the sheets of bark together, but first the roots had to be prepared for sewing. There is an art to removing the bark and splitting the roots so that the result is long, uniform pieces.

First Emma used her knife to split the end of the root, taking care that the split went through the exact center. She then grasped one side of the split root between her teeth, grasped the other half of the root in one hand and the bark in the other. By gently tugging the bark as she pulled the two halves of the roots apart, she was able to peel the bark off as she split the roots. Emma made all this look easy but she did admit that, because you had to work so close to your eyes, it was almost impossible to see what you were doing, so a delicate sense of touch was needed.

Both the peeled and the unpeeled roots have to be kept wet so Emma kept two bowls of water beside her as she worked. The roots will stay pliable longer with the bark left on, so Emma only prepared enough roots for the sewing she intended to do that day.

Emma confidently prepared to start the sewing process. There were no lines marked out to guide the stitching of the pieces of bark together, and the bark, which tended to fight the curves they were trying to impose on it, and bend back against the rows of short pegs. It was hard to see how they would create a canoe from all this, but Noah and Emma worked quietly together guided by their knowledge of age-old traditional building methods.

The important thing at this point was that the sheets under the rock weighted frame were positioned tightly against each other, and sufficiently overlapped to ensure that there was material for the side joints. Once they had the slabs of bark that would be the bottom of the canoe in position, Noah added a dozen more heavy rocks to ensure that nothing would slip out of place while they worked.

As the sheets were forced up between the gunnels and the stakes, they overlapped each other to varying amounts, depending upon the curvature of the canoe at that point. The excess bark was trimmed off before sewing began to produce an even overlap of between one and a half and two inches.

The instrument used to punch the holes for sewing was a short piece of a moose rib bone which had been honed down on a rough rock until it had a smooth sharp point. Note that the point is not round but has a flattened oval cross section. Emma explained that this was the traditional shape for this tool because it made half-circle shaped holes that matched the cross section of the split roots.

Emma also used spruce roots when making baskets. The stitches used in basket making have to be close and very tight, and the shaped holes made by her bone punch made this possible. She did not use such fine stitching on the canoe as she felt that if there were too many holes it would weaken the bark, and in any case waterproofing would be done later with spruce gum.

When sewing, Emma only punched a few holes ahead of where she was actually working as the tightening of the stitches sometimes forced small adjustments of the bark which would put a long row of holes out of line.

As long as the bark was fresh and not dried out, it took only a moderate pressure to make the holes.

The first few stitches were difficult as the bark was only held in position by the pegs driven into the ground, the rock loaded temporary frame and the pressure of the twisted rope on the long uprights.

Noah and Emma were very careful about the placement of the first few stitches. Birch bark, while flexible, has absolutely no give or stretch to it. This means that right from the start the seams made by stitching the bark must be placed precisely where they will remain.

For most of the work, the stitches ran parallel to the seam, each stitch about three-quarters of an inch long, although stitch length and placing did vary to accommodate places where the supporting stakes were placed awkwardly, or particular pieces of bark needed to have stitches that forced the edges into place.

The seams were sewn as tight as possible, but the main concern was strength. No attempt was made at lock stitching as the roots, very pliable when fresh and wet, harden to the stiffness of wood when dry and will not slip.

Noah's Last Canoe

An exterior view of the stitching showing how the entry and exit of the split root uses the same punched hole wherever possible.

The type of stitching used to pull down the edges of the bark where there was a tendency for the natural curl of the bark to force the seams open.

The bark was not trimmed along the gunnels until most of the side seams had been sewn. The seams pulled together as the sewing progressed so that when the gunnel edges were finally trimmed, the bark lay tight against the frame for the whole length of the boat.

Once the bark was pulled together tightly by the stitches in one area, the short stakes were moved to keep the layers of bark as tightly pressed together as possible.

The temporary frame weighed down with rocks was kept inside the canoe until all the side seams had been sewn, and the frame bound to the bark hull. It was necessary to work fairly quickly at this stage as bark became much less flexible as it dried.

The sun was hot and the bark was starting to dry a bit. Pieces of wet cloth thrown over the work at night helped somewhat, and Noah erected a sun screen of leafy branches to shelter the work site.

While Emma continued sewing the bark cover, Noah began splitting short lengths of spruce into thin boards. These boards would be placed inside the canoe between the ribs and the bark. They served both to distribute the pressure of the ribs evenly on the bark hull, and also to serve as reinforcement to the bark in case of accidents while in use. The boards were not fastened in place but were held against the bark hull by the pressure of the ribs.

Noah smoothed the boards using his 'bent knife' or 'mogatogan'. The bent knife is an all purpose tool in the North used for everything from shaping wooden bowls and spoons to carving the intricate frames of snowshoes. It is thought to have been introduced by European traders as it is very similar to the 'farriers knife' used when shoeing horses. Whatever its origin, it became one of the single most useful tools in the North. Many 'mogatogans' were made by heating up an old file, or a piece of a broken blade, bending and retempering it.

Once Noah had made sufficient boards to line the canoe, the next job was the ribs. The ribs were split from long sections of spruce. Noah would force his axe into the end of the log and then drive it along the opening crack with a chunk of wood. Spruce, when it is green and flexible, will split fairly evenly if the pieces on each side of the split are forced apart gradually and carefully. Each rib was about two to two and one half inches wide and perhaps, once Noah had finished smoothing them with his knife, about one quarter of an inch thick. Aside from making sure that the pieces intended for ribs were more than long enough, careful measurement of length was not necessary at this stage as the method of installing the ribs would take care of that.

Because of the tapering of the canoe, all the ribs had to be different sizes and have different degrees of curvature, with the longest and widest one at the centre of the canoe. At first glance this would seem like an almost insoluble problem, but the ancient canoe makers had worked out a procedure that produced a series of ribs, each one smaller and with a more acute curve, just as the shape of the canoe required.

NOAH'S LAST CANOE

First Noah split a number of thin pieces from a carefully selected spruce tree, and cut them into lengths six to ten inches longer than the distance around the hull at the widest part. Each piece was carved to the required thickness and on one side the edges were rounded a bit. These rounded edges would eventually be uppermost on the floor of the canoe and the rounding would reduce any tendency to splinter.

One of the longest pieces was forced down into the canoe and bent into a shape that conformed to the hull. The top ends of that piece were then tied together so that the curve was retained. Then another of the prepared rib boards was forced down inside the first one. This process was repeated until there were enough ribs to do half of the canoe. In the picture you can see that each rib is smaller and each curve is a bit more acute than the one before it. Two sets of these bundles were produced, one for use from the center to the bow, and one for use from the center to the stern.

Noah's son, Peter, is shown holding one of the 'nests' of ribs. When spruce is first cut, it is very pliable, although great care has to be taken in bending the pieces that make up the smallest and most tightly curved ribs. If you look closely at the bundle of ribs, you will see that small blocks have been placed between some of the ribs to increase the amount of curvature. Near the bow and stern of the canoe, the curve becomes very acute. The blocks help to ensure that the dried ribs will better conform to the shape of the finished canoe. Noah said that the individual ribs would be trimmed to the proper length as they were installed.

After a few days drying while bound into the curve, the ribs would retain their shape. The ribs were always dried well before being installed as they are only held into the boat by their resistance to further bending.

There was no blueprint when the Custers began to build, but generations of their ancestors had left them a plan as carefully crafted as if they had been working from a drawing. They spoke often of the young people who might see their canoe and benefit from the knowledge they had been given. Not much discussion was needed. They worked to the rhythm of age-old custom, often making pieces they would not need until days later, if the piece was going to require drying time for example.

It would be next-to-impossible to bend a piece thick enough for the stem and stern pieces into the required curves, so Noah split the wood into thin slats, which made the pieces relatively easy to bend into the required shape. These curved stem and stern pieces were tightly bound and left to dry. In the photograph Peter is holding the stern piece; another identical piece was made for the bow. Once dry, they maintained their shape and the lashing of the bark hull over them made the curvature permanent.

Note that bark canoes of this type have no keel so there is no direct wood connection between the bottom end of the stem and stern pieces. They rely on the strength of the curved bark and the tension of the ribs.

As word began to get around that what could be the last traditional family-built canoe to be made by the Woodland Cree was taking shape on the banks of the Sturgeon Weir River, the Custers began to get a lot of visitors.

Most of the time people were content to watch, take pictures and ask questions. Usually Peter or Anna, who were both more comfortable in English than either Noah or Emma, would provide the explanations.

Cree hospitality is legendary and often work on the canoe would be suspended for a time, while Noah and Emma attended to their guests. They were both very conscious of the fact that they were passing on a skill learned at the feet of their elders and did not begrudge the time to explain what they were doing.

My daughters, Sandra and Elizabeth, often accompanied me on trips out to see how the canoe was progressing. I was always very pleased that they had this opportunity to learn and to share something of the wisdom of the First Nations people.

NOAH'S LAST CANOE

With the stitching on the sides of the canoe done, it was time to trim the bark along the gunnels and bind it to the frame.

This was another part of the construction process where the work required a fair amount of art. There were no ribs in the boat at this stage so the only thing holding the bark anywhere near its future shape was the temporary frame inside and the pegs and posts outside.

Noah and Emma worked side by side, one pressing the bark into a position as close as possible to the final desired shape, and the other scoring a line along the edge of the frame where the bark would be cut.

In the picture you can see that the Custers only trimmed a limited amount of the bark along the frame before binding it, to ensure that the tightening of the binding did not cause the bark to move on the frame.

In the background of one of these pictures you can see the frame of the twelve-foot canoe which Noah had proposed first.

The first step in canoe building traditionally is to build the frame. Since the frame governs the canoe's final shape and size, it acts as a template, and enables one to get some idea of what the new canoe will be like. With the frame on the ground you could imagine yourself sitting in it, imagine where your wife would sit and where you would put your children, your packs and equipment.

In the case of the Museum canoe, since we did not want to inadvertently introduce any non-Cree ideas about what a canoe should look like, no comment was made on the shape Noah was proposing to build, but the Museum had asked for a canoe at least sixteen feet long. Noah agreed to the length and set out to build a canoe as he thought it should be built.

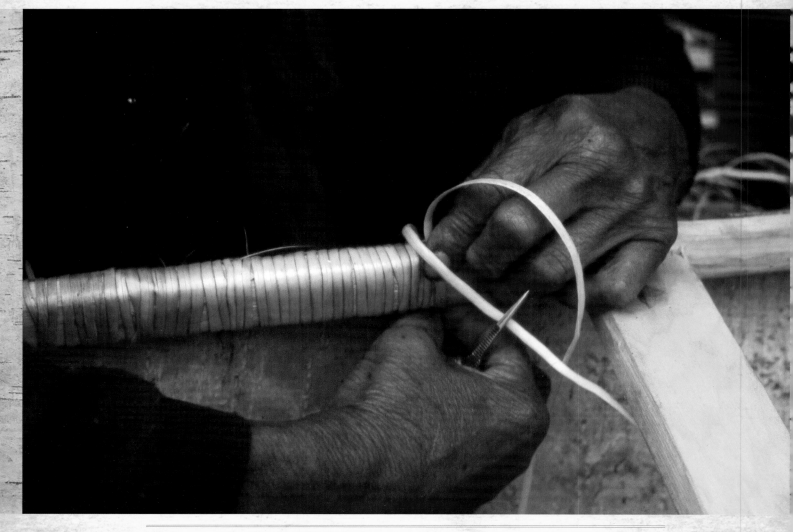

In the picture you can see the metal punch Noah liked to use. It did not make the same traditional half-moon shaped hole that Emma's punch made but it did take less effort to pierce the bark.

Where the bark was being bound to the frame, the roots were closely spaced forming a solid cover over the frame and the edge of the bark. The holes in the bark were punched in a staggered pattern so that the closely spaced holes would not weaken the bark. As with much of this ancient technology, a very practical solution to a problem also produced a very artistic finish. The drawing illustrates the arrangement of the holes that permits the binding to be very close without tearing the bark.

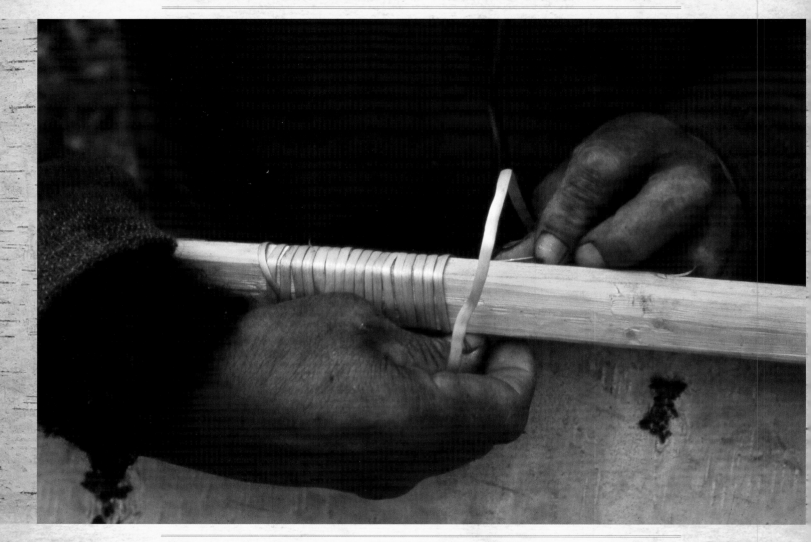

Sewing the sides of the canoe to the frame was a time-consuming process. Each turn of the binding progressed along the length of the canoe by the width of a spruce root, so the work was slow and the necessity of ensuring that the shape of the canoe was maintained made this part of the work very painstaking.

It was at this stage that the holes in the thwart were used. When the binding reached the point where a thwart met the gunnel, the roots were passed through the holes to lock the thwart solidly to the frame.

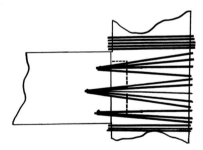

*... if the canoe felt that it looked good,
it would "walk on the water"*

Once the frame had been bound to the hull, the stem and stern pieces were tied to the end of the frame and then the same binding process was used to attach them firmly to the bark of the hull.

When this process was complete, and before the rocks and temporary frame were removed from the canoe, a thin slat was bound to the gunnels of the canoe to protect the stitching from the rub of paddles or other damage.

Noah then took a piece of bark and carefully separated the layers to expose the rich dark colour of the inner bark. From this he made a piece to fit over the binding that held the stem and stern pieces to the frame. When asked about the function of this particular piece, Noah said that it was just to make the canoe look good. He said that if the canoe felt that it looked good, it would "walk on the water" with more confidence.

NOAH'S LAST CANOE

In this picture you can see the finished bow of the canoe. All the different kinds of stitching are evident here, including the staggered pattern used when binding the hull to the frame.

The method of splitting large pieces that have to be bent was used here on the protective strips.

Historic pictures and paintings show that the Cree canoe did not have the high recurved bow that was typical of the Eastern canoe. The craft that Noah was producing fitted very closely with what was known of the typical Woodland Cree canoe.

Noah's Last Canoe

Once all the binding work was done on the frame as well as the bow and stern pieces, the temporary frame and the rocks that held it down could at last be removed and the canoe lifted up so that the bottom seams could be sewn.

Sewing these seams was a difficult operation because it was hard to reach across the wider parts of the hull to put the stitches in. In spite of their best efforts, the bark was beginning to dry a bit and getting hard to work with, but Noah and Emma worked together punching holes and passing the split roots back and forth.

As the ribs and liner boards were not yet installed, the canoe looked like a big misshapen bag, but careful adherence to the traditional building methods would ensure that the canoe would be well-proportioned when it was finished.

NOAH'S LAST CANOE

At this stage the canoe consisted only of the frame and the bark hull. It would require the installation of the ribs to give it strength and shape. Between the ribs and the hull, Noah placed a layer of thin flat boards made by splitting spruce poles into thin slats and smoothing them with his bent knife.

The green lines represent the ends of these boards and show how Noah used them to cover the whole of the bark hull. The boards were not fastened in but would depend on the pressure of the ribs to hold them in place.

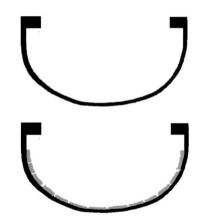

The tied bundles of ribs had dried and were much less flexible than they had been. They had become somewhat springy and would try to resume their shape if bent further. Starting with the largest rib from one of the bundles, Noah began work at the center of the canoe. One end of a rib would be placed under the frame on one side. Then, placing a small notched piece of wood on the other end of the rib, Noah hammered the rib down into the canoe with a wooden hammer until it was tight against the boards.

When the rib had been driven in tight, it was marked at the frame and cut off. Then the same notched piece of wood and the hammer were used to drive it in again until the cut end snapped under the frame. The red arrow in the drawing shows this movement. Driving the rib in this way stretches the bark very tight. There were no fastenings; the ribs were held in by their pressure against the frame and the boards were held in by the ribs.

NOAH'S LAST CANOE

Noah is shown here with his hammer. He had just driven the last rib home and was surveying his handiwork. In the bow and stern of the canoe, where the curve required was so acute that the ribs could not be bent to fit, a small flat board was inserted between the sides of the frame on top and the bottom end of the stem and stern pieces.

These boards served the same function as the ribs in holding the liner boards and the bark hull in position, and they also provided support to the bottom end of the stem and stern pieces, transferring the shock of hitting something to the frame.

At this stage, the canoe still looked a bit misshapen. The natural irregularities of the bark would have to be adjusted for. To make these corrections, Noah would sit for a while studying the canoe in order to determine which rib was exerting too much or not enough pressure. One or two of the offending ribs were removed and shortened a bit and then pounded back in. In the case of two ribs near the center of the canoe that were not tight enough, Noah slipped extra boards under them to increase the pressure on the bark.

According to Noah, all this attention to detail was important in order to insure that the canoe, in his words, "would swim straight".

As the minor adjustments proceeded, the true beauty of the birch canoe began to appear. That this remarkable craft could be built with simple tools, using materials gathered from the bush around the camp, was wonderful to see. Elegant, fast, strong and reliable, the bark canoe was one of the finest examples of the technology of the First Nations people and it was not equaled anywhere in the world.

Noah and Emma Custer, with the help of their children Peter and Anna, had brought the traditional Woodland Cree canoe back to life. Perhaps this would be the last canoe built in the old way by a family living in their summer camp by the river.

Noah said that it was over half a century since, as a small boy, he had helped with the construction of the last one. Fifty years is a long time, but from the sure and certain way that Noah and Emma worked, it was evident that they had carefully treasured their inheritance.

Noah's Last Canoe

The basic construction work was finished. All through the process of gathering materials and building the canoe, it was evident that some things were done by the men, some were the responsibility of the women, and some tasks were shared.

Noah and his son had done all the wood cutting, and forming of the frame, liner boards and ribs, as well as their installation. I asked Noah if there was some fixed rule about who carried out each task but he said simply that as far as he knew "it had always been done that way".

Emma and her daughter Anna had gathered, peeled and split all the roots. They also prepared the bark once it had been harvested and saw to it being carefully stored in the water. After the actual construction of the canoe was finished, it was Emma who gathered and prepared the spruce gum, and applied it to waterproof the seams.

The job of sewing was shared between Emma and Noah.

During the construction stage the attention of the builders is concentrated almost totally on the shape and strength of the craft. Although the seams are made as close and tight as possible, actual waterproofing of the hull is accomplished only after the canoe is complete.

Up to this point the canoe had been worked on lying right side up, but now it was time to turn it over so work could begin on the waterproofing of the seams.

Watching Noah and Peter handling the new canoe, I was struck by the fact that, although the Woodland Cree did not build huge stone temples and pyramids like the Maya, or enigmatic stone cities like the Inca, they had left an even more enduring monument to their skills. Even when constructed from exotic twentieth century fibers and resins, the timeless design of the canoe remained as a tribute to the First Nations people.

Noah's Last Canoe

Surveying the lines of the bottom of the canoe, Noah found one or two spots where the bark wasn't stretched just to his liking, and more work was done adjusting ribs and liner boards until he was satisfied.

Even after all this work there were still a few small wrinkles in the bark, most of them from the original shape of the bark on the tree. Noah said that these would flatten out in time as the bark dried and tightened around the frame and the ribs.

It is worth noting that the bark canoe could easily be repaired. If a hole was punched in the hull, a piece could be sewn over the damaged area and sealed with pitch made from spruce gum and grease. Broken liner boards and even ribs could be replaced in the field. Since the canoe itself was quite resilient, it was not common that the frame itself would be broken, but even in such cases, reinforcing pieces could be bound over the damage.

It was not necessary to carry a repair kit of any kind, since all the necessary material could be found almost anywhere in the Woodland Crees' traditional area, and the tools needed were the common implements of everyday life.

Noah's Last Canoe

One day Noah sat for a long time studying the canoe. He said he was watching it swim and looking for any bad habits it might have. After a while he pronounced himself satisfied.

At this stage the canoe, although elegant looking, was not water tight. The spruce root stitching, tight and very strong, was not expected to produce leak-proof seams. Holes made for the split roots and the natural irregularities of the bark meant that a waterproof coating of pitch would have to be applied to all the sewn joints.

For a few days, while Noah was installing the liner boards and ribs, Emma and Anna had been gathering the spruce gum that would be required for the next step in the process.

Wherever a spruce tree's bark has been damaged, by the wind breaking a limb, or by woodpeckers seeking grubs, the tree exudes a sticky sap to heal the wound. This sap thickens to a hard amber-like substance as it dries. Emma said that the best place to look for spruce gum was on the older trees, especially those near the lakeshore that would have been more exposed to storms and suffered more broken branches and bark damage.

Emma had collected a quantity of this material. At first it looked as if she had vastly overestimated how much gum she would need to waterproof the seams of the canoe, but spruce gum harvested in this manner has a lot of bark in it. The challenge here was to separate the gum from the bark. To ensure that it would conform closely to the shape of the bark and also penetrate the seams, the gum had to be free of all but the smallest particles of bark. It was important that the gum remain on the heat until any entrapped moisture was boiled out of it.

Once again there was a demonstration of ancient technical know-how. Melted spruce gum is too thick to pour through a screen to sieve the bits of bark out of it, but the Cree long ago devised a solution to the problem.

Noah made a small hoop that fit in the gum pot and wove a screen or net inside the hoop using the same cross weave pattern used when making snowshoes. When the bark was sufficiently hot to be soft and runny, the hoop was placed on top of the mass of melted gum and bark in the pot, and pressed down, taking all the bark to the bottom of the pot.

Spruce gum at this stage is quite liquid and has a consistency similar to warm honey, but it is not yet suitable for waterproofing the seams of the canoe. The problem is that when the gum cools it becomes very brittle and glassy, and the working of the hull of the canoe in the waves would cause it to crumble and crack off, leaving the seams open to the water. Once again traditional knowledge had a solution.

An amount of melted gum, equal to what Mrs. Custer could use before it got too cool to work with, was poured into an old frying pan. The reason for this extra process soon became clear. If a certain amount of oil or grease is mixed with the hot gum, the result is a substance that has the properties of tar. It is sticky and waterproof but does not become brittle in the coldest water.

In early times, the Cree would boil quantities of fish, drying the meal as a winter food supply and storing the oil in bottles made of fish skin. This fish oil was used to render the spruce gum pliable.

Lacking the traditional fish oil, Emma substituted bacon grease, which seemed to work just fine.

Hot spruce gum is difficult to work, and will give a nasty burn if you aren't careful, as the bubbling hot gum sticks to the skin. Using only a flat stick, Emma began at the bow of the canoe, working the hot gum into each seam and smearing a generous quantity of it over the exposed stitches. Gum that was too hot could run a bit as can be seen in the photo. This made the operation look a bit messy as the black gum stood out starkly against the light bark. Emma said she did like to make neat-looking work, but considered it more important that the seams be waterproof. The gum had to be as hot as possible to ensure good penetration of all the seams and sewing holes.

NOAH'S LAST CANOE

This picture perhaps give the best illustration of the layout of the bark hull. The number of pieces of bark would not be many less than shown here, even if the slabs were from bigger trees and therefore somewhat wider. It would still be necessary to fit additional pieces just below the frame. On the first piece of bark directly behind the bow you can see where Emma has applied gum to the gussets cut in the bottom panel to accommodate the increasingly acute curve of the hull.

The work was painstaking but Emma kept at it. She could only prepare a small amount of gum at a time as it quickly cooled below the temperature at which it would make a satisfactory seal. About a cup of hot spruce gum at a time was added to the pan and a bit more than a large tablespoon full of grease or oil was mixed in. I asked Emma if there was a traditional proportion of oil to spruce gum that produced the best results, but she said the different gums and different greases all produced different results so you had to experiment a bit.

Noah's Last Canoe

At last the job of applying the spruce gum was finished. Noah and Emma went over the new canoe inch by inch, and pronounced it ready for the water.

The canoe was outfitted with two paddles made from spruce planks split from a log using the same technique as that used in making the ribs and liner boards. A length of rope was made from the bark of a willow that grows along the river bank. This willow bark was used for making things like fishing nets. It was very strong but had to be kept moist as it became brittle when dry. There were no seats because the Cree paddler was either sitting on something in the bottom of the canoe or kneeling.

Noah's Last Canoe

"this was a canoe that would swim straight and not be afraid of waves."

What the Custers had produced was a traditional Cree canoe. Tough, utilitarian and made entirely of materials found within half a mile of the camp. The team effort of a family could produce a canoe of this type in two weeks of concentrated work.

The canoe was launched into the water in the reeds by the shore and allowed to drift around for a while. Noah followed it in his own canoe and from time to time would give it a push this way and that so he could observe its behavior. Satisfied at last, he announced that "this was a canoe that would swim straight and not be afraid of waves."

NOAH'S LAST CANOE

The bark canoe built by Noah and Emma Custer is now in The Manitoba Museum.

The Custers built the canoe using designs and methods recalled from their childhood. It is a very reliable example of the type of canoe traditional to the Woodland Cree.

The canoe is a treasure come down to us from a rich and ancient culture.

It is also a memorial to Noah and Emma who chose to live as their ancestors had lived.